7-18-07

Auto Racing

Tony Norman

GARETH**STEVENS**
GS
PUBLISHING
A Member of the WRC Media Family of Companies

Please visit our web site at: **www.garethstevens.com**
For a free color catalog describing Gareth Stevens Publishing's
list of high-quality books and multimedia programs, call
1-800-542-2595 (USA) or 1-800-387-3178 (Canada).
Gareth Stevens Publishing's fax: (414) 332-3567.

Library of Congress Cataloging-in-Publication Data

Norman, Tony.
    Auto racing / Tony Norman.
      p. cm. — (Action sports)
    ISBN 0-8368-6365-8 (lib. bdg.)
    1. Automobile racing—Juvenile literature. I. Title. II. Action sports (Milwaukee, Wis.)
  GV1029.13.N67   2006
  796.72—dc22
                                        2005044710

This edition first published in 2006 by
Gareth Stevens Publishing
A Member of the WRC Media Family of Companies
330 West Olive Street, Suite 100
Milwaukee, Wisconsin 53212 USA

Gareth Stevens editor: Carol Ryback
Gareth Stevens designer: Scott M. Krall

Picture credits: (t)=top; (b)=bottom; (c)=center; (l)=left; (r)=right)
Shell: 3, 5(tl), 5(cl),12(b), 13(t), 14(b), 16(b). Autostock: 8(b), 9(t),10(b).
Chris Wright, www.bangerracing.com/: 5(tr), 26–27. Honda 19.
Alamy: / Mark Scott 11(t); / Transtock Inc. 21(t). U.S. Army: 4(r), 5(br),
5(bl), 7(t), 18(b), 21(bl), 21(br), 22(b).

Printed in the United States of America

1 2 3 4 5 6 7 8 9 10 09 08 07 06

Contents

Introduction

People all over the world are passionate about car racing. Some cars are built especially for racing, while others look just like the normal cars that people drive around in everyday. Racers also drive "beater" cars and trucks and funny-looking cars that make people laugh.

Born in the USA

NASCAR (National Association for Stock Car Auto Racing) and drag racing both began in the United States. NASCAR racetracks have high, sloping banks. Drag racing cars take off almost like rockets. Cars compete to reach the fastest speed on a 0.25-mile (400 meter) track.

A Formula One driver must squeeze into a small cockpit.

Racing across the world

Like all race cars, Formula One cars are single-seat racers. In 2005, twenty-two drivers from fourteen countries raced at nineteen different Grand Prix circuits, or racetracks, around the globe.

NASCAR

Formula One facts - Did you know?

Most of the controls and gauges for Formula One cars are on the steering wheel. Drivers find fingertip controls quicker and safer than foot pedals.

Formula One

Pit Crew

Drag Racing

Demolition Derby

Drivers must wear helmets and fire-resistant clothes.

The bright colors and logos on race cars make it easy for fans to watch their favorite car.

NASCAR

NASCAR races are some the most popular sporting events in the United States. The first NASCAR race was held near Charlotte, North Carolina, in 1948. Now, more than eighteen hundred NASCAR races occur at tracks all over the United States every year. Florida's Daytona 500 is one of NASCAR's most important events.

Devoted fans

NASCAR races draw huge crowds of more than 185,000 spectators, but this is only a small fraction of the number of fans. Millions of people in the U.S. and in more than 150 other countries follow the races on TV.

The races

The NASCAR race season lasts from February to November. The most important races are part of the premier series, named the Nextel Cup series, after Nextel, its sponsor. There is also the Busch Series for young drivers and the Craftsman Truck Series for pickup trucks.

NASCAR facts - Did you know?

It takes about one hundred twenty hours to build an engine for a Nextel Cup or Busch Series race car. Mechanics spend about forty hours cleaning and tuning an engine after a race.

Greg Biffle won the 2005 Nextel race at the Texas Motor Speedway in Fort Worth, Texas.

TRUE STORIES

Dale Earnhardt was one of NASCAR's best drivers. He had seventy-six career wins and won a race on every major U.S. racetrack. Dale died in a crash during the 2001 Daytona 500 in Florida. His son, Dale Earnhardt Junior, is now a top NASCAR driver.

The NASCAR rules state that all cars must be "American-made steel-bodied passenger sedans."

Daytona International Speedway in Florida.
One lap: 2.5 miles (4 kilometers)

Bristol Motor Speedway in Tennessee.
One lap: 0.5 miles (0.8 km)

California State Speedway in Fontana.
One lap: 2 miles (3.2 km)

On the Racetrack

The Nextel Cup circuit, NASCAR's top series, consists of thirty-six events at racetracks all over the U.S. Each race has a set distance. Cars speed around the track until they complete the full distance of the race. Some races are 600 miles (965 km) long and last many hours.

Championship point

The first-place finisher for each race wins 180 points. Second place is worth 170 points, and third place is worth 165 points. Drivers get five points for each lap they lead, as well as a five-point bonus for leading the most laps in a race. The driver who earns the most total points in the thirty-six races is declared the overall series champion.

Each vehicle is inspected before a race to ensure it complies with NASCAR rules.

In the groove

"High groove" racers stay at the top of the banked slope of the racetrack to keep a steady speed and avoid slower cars. "Low groove" drivers prefer to race low on the slope on the inside of the track.

NASCAR facts - Did you know?

Cars often drive nose-to-tail, just a few inches apart. Drivers like to ride in the slipstream created by the car immediately in front of them. This maneuver is called "drafting."

Cars can reach speeds of more than 212 miles (340 km) per hour.

TRUE STORIES

Talladega, Alabama, 1997. One of the worst ever NASCAR crashes occurred at the Talladega racetrack. Twenty-seven cars were involved, and many were destroyed, but no drivers were badly hurt.

Gateway International Raceway Madison, Illinois. One lap: 1.25 miles (2 km)

Darlington Raceway in South Carolina. One lap: 1.3 miles (2.1 km)

Talladega Superspeedway in Alabama. One lap: 2.6 miles (4.2 km)

Cars and Drivers

When **NASCAR** racing began, competitors drove ordinary cars that had been modified for racing. Now, **NASCAR** race cars are specially built by experts. It takes ten days just to make the car's body from sheet metal.

Safety gear

Most NASCAR drivers wear full-face helmets that cover the head and face. These helmets weigh 3 pounds (1.3 kilograms) but can feel five times heavier as the cars race around the steep banks of the track. Drivers wear seatbelts and have a head and neck support in case of crashes. Drivers must be in top physical shape to cope with the demands of the race.

Top teams

More than thirty teams take part in the Nextel Cup Series. Top teams may have five drivers racing for them during the season. Smaller teams have just one driver.

The Nextel All-Star Challenge is only open to the winners from the current and previous racing seasons.

NASCAR facts - Did you know?

Engineers use "horsepower" units to measure a car's engine power. NASCAR car engines are rated at 750 horsepower: the same amount of power as generated by 750 horses!

While female NASCAR drivers are rare, a few of them compete in the Craftsman Truck series.

TRUE STORIES

Pocono Raceway, Pennsylvania, 2003. NASCAR star racer Dale Jarrett's car crashed and burst into flames. Dale jumped out and ran to safety.

Memphis Motorsports Park in Tennessee.
One lap: 0.75 miles (1.2 km)

Kansas Speedway in Kansas City.
One lap: 1.5 miles (2.4 km)

Texas Motor Speedway in Fort Worth.
One lap: 1.5 miles (2.4 km)

Formula One

The first Formula One World Championship race was at Silverstone, Northamptonshire, England, on May 18, 1950. Nineteen worldwide Formula One races – now called Grand Prix (French for "big prize") – are held annually. Grand Prix races are about 190 miles (300 km) long.

Cost of a car

Millions of dollars go into designing and building a Formula One car. The costliest part is the body design. The engine and other parts, such as the steering wheel and seat, also cost many thousands of dollars.

Feel the heat

A Formula One race lasts about one and one-half hours. Temperatures inside the car often reach 140 °Fahrenheit (60 °Celsius). The drivers sometimes lose 12 pounds (5.4 kg) during a race because they sweat so much. Many drivers drink water or sports drinks through a plastic tube linked to their race helmet as they race around.

Drivers sit in the "survival cell." It must meet strict regulations to protect the driver in a crash.

Formula One facts – Did you know?

The Grand Prix race in the tiny country of Monaco does not occur on a racetrack. Instead, cars race on the streets of Monte Carlo, which have many twists and turns and few chances for drivers to pass one another.

Successful passing requires powerful acceleration and skillful braking.

TRUE STORIES

Dallas, Texas, Grand Prix 1984.
English driver Nigel Mansell ran out of gas near the end of the race. Nigel tried to push his car over the finish line to win points but collapsed in the 108 °F (42 °C) heat.

Kuala Lumpur, Malaysia
One lap: 3.4 miles (5.5 km)
Number of laps: 56

Sao Paulo, Brazil
One lap: 2.6 miles
(4.3 km) 71 laps.

Melbourne, Australia
One lap: 3.3 miles (5.3km)
Number of laps: 58

High-Speed Races

Formula One races are run on Grand Prix racetracks in countries all over the world. Almost fifty racetracks were built to Grand Prix standards, including nine in the United States. Each racetrack has a different design, and each track is a different length.

Starting grid

The cars line up in rows. Each row has two cars. Lights on a stand above the track tell the drivers when to start. Drivers do time trials, or practice laps, the day before a race. The fastest driver goes to the front of the starting grid. This is called "pole position."

How to win

Pole position is good because drivers want to start in the lead. Passing is very difficult on most Formula One tracks because of the many turns. Some drivers try to pass when other cars slow down to go around a turn. The higher the speed, the harder it is to control the car, and the more dangerous passing becomes.

The helmets worn by Grand Prix drivers are hooked to a supply of compressed air. Drivers breathe this air if their car starts on fire.

Formula One facts – Did you know?

Zandvoort, the Netherlands, 1961. Fifteen cars started in the Dutch Grand Prix — and fifteen cars finished. It is the only Formula One race where no cars dropped out.

UNITED STATES GRAND PRIX
INDIANAPOLIS

Cars leave the starting grid in the U.S. Grand Prix in Indianapolis, Indiana.

TRUE STORIES

Nürburgring Grand Prix, Germany, 1976. Niki Lauda's car crashed and burst into flames. Niki suffered serious burns and broken bones. Despite his injuries, he was back racing just six weeks later.

At the very beginning of a Formula One race, a safety car follows behind to ensure that the race gets off to a safe start.

Catalunya, Spain
One circuit: 2.8 miles (4.6 km)
Number of laps: 66

Magny-Cours, France
One lap: 2.7 miles (4.4 km)
Number of laps: 70

Silverstone, England
One lap: 3.1 miles (5.1 km)
Number of laps: 60

Team Tactics

Grand Prix drivers compete for their teams and for themselves. The winner of each race is awarded ten points, plus ten points for the team. The driver and team in second place get eight points, with the third-place driver and team getting six points. At the end of the season, the driver with the most points becomes world champion.

Teams

Each Grand Prix team enters two cars in every race. Teams may have up to five different drivers. The teams are named after the company that sponsors them. The sponsors of race teams advertise their companies by using "signature" colors and logos on the race cars and on clothing worn by the team.

Drivers

Drivers wear fireproof jumpsuits, boots, gloves, underwear, and hoods called balaclavas. Shoulder straps on the jumpsuits make it easier for the safety teams to remove a driver from a car in case of a crash. The lightweight, special materials in the helmets can withstand strong forces.

Brazilian driver Rubens Barrichello races for the Ferrari team.

Formula One facts - Did you know?

Germany's Michael Schumacher was the first Formula One driver to become world champion seven times. He took the title in 1994, 1995, 2000, 2001, 2002, 2003, and 2004.

TRUE STORIES
Graham Hill was a Formula One world champion who died six months after retiring from racing in 1975. His son, Damon, became a Grand Prix star, too, and won the world championship in 1996.

Formula One cars are built low to the ground to reduce air turbulence (drag), which slows cars down.

Spa, Belgium
One lap: 4.2 miles (6.9 km)
Number of laps: 44

Montreal, Canada
One lap: 2.6 miles (4.3 km)
Number of laps: 70

Indianapolis, Indiana
One lap: 2.5 miles (4.1 km)
Number of laps: 73

In the Pits

NASCAR and Formula One teams have their own mechanics. The mechanics work in a safe area next to the racetrack called the pits. Drivers and pit crews communicate by radio during races.

NASCAR pits

A crew chief leads the NASCAR pit crew. It takes a pit crew less than twenty seconds to pump in 22 gallons (83 liters) of fuel and change all four tires. Tires get so hot during a race that the rubber gets tacky. This helps the car grip the racetrack surface.

Formula One pits

Formula One cars may only change a set of tires if it rains. Cars average two pit stops per race to refuel. Two men pump fuel into the car at a rate of 3 gallons (12 L) per second. Pit stops only last about six to twelve seconds. A Formula One car uses about 35 gallons (130 L) of gasoline in a race.

NASCAR allows only seven mechanics in the pits during a race.

Racing facts - Did you know?

A racing car's "black box" is a computer that records engine data, much like the black box on an airplane. It sends the information to the pit crew during the race.

Action Sports | 19

TRUE STORIES

Formula One teams spend millions of dollars a year moving their cars to the different racetracks around the world. Each truck also carries 100 gallons (380 L) of fuel.

A Formula One car makes a pit stop to refuel.

NASCAR and Formula One races use these flags:

Race completed.

All cars must stop.

Danger ahead. Passing is not allowed.

Driver must make a pit stop.

Drag Racing

Drag racing started on the dry lake beds of California in the 1930s. At first, dragsters were just street cars with parts of the body stripped away to make them go faster. They were nicknamed "hot rods." The first legal hot rod races began in 1953.

How the race is won

The object of drag racing is to go as fast as possible over a short, straight course for about 0.25 miles (400 m). Two cars compete in each "heat" of a drag race. The winner of each heat goes into the next round of the contest. The last two cars left compete for the top prize.

Official organizations

The National Hot Rod Association (NHRA) organizes most of the drag racing events in North America. Every year, it holds more than five thousand events at one hundred forty tracks. The International Hot Rod Association (IHRA) has different rules than the NHRA. Most IHRA races are only 0.12 miles (200 m) long.

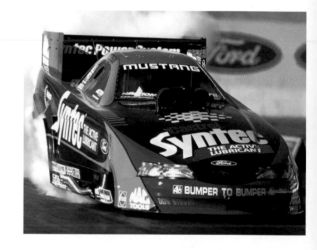

Some drag racing cars are built only for use on the racetrack.

Drag racing facts - Did you know?

A drag racer can accelerate from zero to 300 miles (480 km) per hour in 4.5 seconds — faster than a jumbo jet accelerates.

TRUE STORIES

Top Fuel drag racing star Doug Kalitta from Ypsilanti, Michigan, is also a skilled pilot. By age twenty-one, he could fly a Lear jet. He was one of the youngest Lear jet pilots ever.

Only *two* hot rods race in each heat.

The body of a Top Fuel drag car is long and thin to reduce air resistance.

The brakes of a drag car produce so much heat that the tires smoke.

The rear wheels of a Top Fuel drag car wear out after only four to six races.

Dragster Classes

Professional and amateur drag racers use more than two hundred kinds of vehicles. Young drivers between the ages of eight and seventeen compete in Junior Dragsters races. Street Car races give fans a chance to race their own cars on local, and sometimes famous, racetracks.

Top three
Professional drag racing has three main classes:

Top Fuel dragsters are the elite racers. They can go from 0 to 100 miles (0 to 160 km) per hour in less than one second. In races, speeds might top 330 miles (530 km) per hour.

Funny Cars are drag racers with brightly-colored fiberglass bodies and big, "funny" rear wheels. They can hit top speeds of more than 300 miles (480 km) per hour.

Pro-stock cars look somewhat like regular car models, but their high-powered engines give them a top speed of more than 200 miles (320 km) per hour.

The engine of a Top Fuel dragster is at the back of the car.

Drag racing facts - Did you know?
Mechanics take apart dragster engines after every race and change many of the parts. One race for a Top Fuel dragster may cost several thousand dollars.

TRUE STORIES
Don Garlits is nicknamed drag racing's "Big Daddy." Don built thirty-four race cars, all called "Swamp Rat." He was the first man to top 250 miles (402 km) per hour. He won 144 major events.

Pro-stock cars are highly modified versions of car models that people might drive for personal use.

Large rear wheels make the body of a Funny Car look as if it is tilting forward.

Funny Cars have rear-wheel drives. The engine is in front.

A Funny Car's engine must conform to certain specifications.

Drag-Car Power

Associations that organize drag races make rules about what drivers may do to their cars. The rules list what changes a driver can make to a car's engine, brakes, body style, and other features. Many rules are meant to keep the drivers, spectators, and mechanics safe.

Feel the power

Top Fuel dragster engines have forty times the power of most cars — more than 8,000 horsepower. Instead of gasoline, the dragsters use high-power racing alcohol for fuel. Pit crews test the engines for forty-five minutes before a race. The noise is deafening, and the pit crews must wear ear protection.

Burnout

Before a race, the driver takes the car to an area called the "Burnout Box." As water is sprayed onto the tires, the driver spins the tires to warm them up — while applying the brakes at the same time. The tires get so warm they smoke or "burn out." After the burnout, the tires grip the track better.

Top Fuel cars use drag chutes to slow down after a race.

Drag racing facts - Did you know?

NASCAR and Formula One rules ban fans from being inside the pits during races. Spectators can, however, stand just a few feet away and watch as pit crews work on the cars.

The body of a Funny Car covers the wheels to reduce wind resistance.

TRUE STORIES

Gainsville, Florida, 1992: Kenny Bernstein was the first drag racer to top 300 miles (482 km) per hour. In 2004, Kenny's son, Brandon, hit 333 miles (535 km) per hour in a Top Fuel dragster — a new world record.

Pro-stock car lights must remain in the original factory position.

An air intake on the "bonnet" draws air into the engine.

Pro-stock cars must use special racing gasoline.

Crash!

Most racing cars are kept in great condition, with gleaming paint jobs, but a car contest called a demolition derby uses cars that are ready for the junkyard. The whole point of a demolition derby is for drivers to crash into the other cars on purpose!

Derby safety

Demolition drivers make their cars as safe as possible by removing all the glass, the radio, and everything else inside the car except for a driver's seat. Drivers also change the location of the gas tank to help avoid an explosion or fire from gasoline.

Last one moving wins

Demolition derbies are popular throughout the United States. Cars do not race along a track. They just smash into each other, usually while driving backward over mud. The last car still running at the end wins. The British version of a demolition derby is called a banger race. The cars race around a track while crashing together.

Demolition derbies use a muddy field. The mud keeps speeds down.

Demolition derby facts - Did you know?

Drivers do not only use cars in demolition derby competitions. They also might drive trucks, tractors, school buses — or even lawn mowers!

TRUE STORIES

Franklin, Wisconsin, 1950. Used car dealer "Crazy Jim" Groh sponsors the first demolition derby. In 1974, ABC TV's *Wide World of Sports* introduces demolition derbies to the nation.

British banger cars crash into each other as they race toward the finish line.

Safety precautions help prevent serious injuries.

Most demolition or banger drivers are amateurs who enter contests just for fun.

Drivers remove all glass from their demolition derby cars.

Around the World

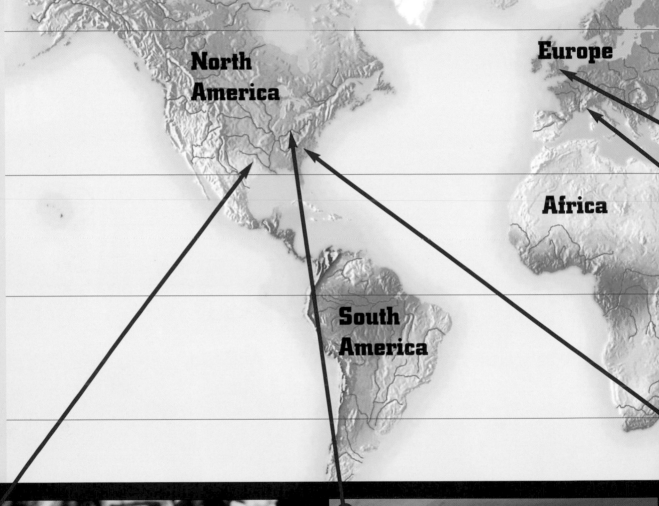

North
America

Europe

Africa

South
America

Ennis, Texas – the Texas Multiplex holds many drag car racing events, including pro-stock races.

Indianapolis, Indiana – the Indianapolis 500 is held at the Indianapolis Motor Speedway.

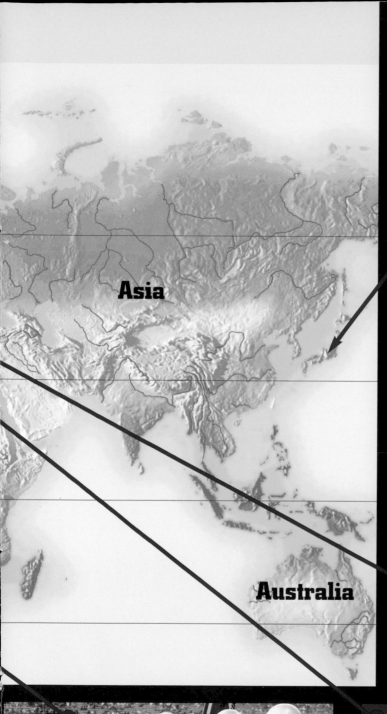

Asia

Australia

Suzuka, Japan – host to the Japanese Formula One Grand Prix since 1987.

Silverstone, England – the site of the first Formula One race still hosts Grand Prix races.

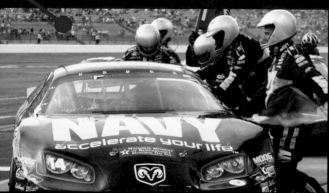

Concord, North Carolina – workers tend to a car during a pit stop at Lowe's Motor Speedway.

Monte Carlo, Monaco – the Formula One Grand Prix is held on city streets.

Glossary

amateur: someone who does something for fun.

balaclavas: fabric hoods.

banks: sloping sides.

beater: a slang term for an older car that is ready for the junkyard.

bonnet: the hood of a car.

burnout: the smoke created by spinning the wheels to heat the rubber of the tires so they grip the track better.

championship: a main competition. The winner is called the champion.

checkered: patterned in squares of two colors, usually black and white. A checkered flag signals the end of a race.

cockpit: a small area for the driver or pilot.

drafting: riding close behind a leading car to take advantage of the reduced air flow, or slipstream, which can add speed and reduce gasoline use.

dragster: a drag-racing car.

elite: the best of its type.

fiberglass: a type of spun glass made into crisscrossing fibers that form a lightweight material often used in race-car bodies.

Formula One: races that feature cars with open cockpits and in which the engine is behind the driver.

funny car: a type of fast drag car with extremely large rear wheels.

Grand Prix: French for "big prize." This series of major races originated in France.

heat: another name for an individual segment of a race within a larger race that helps determine which racers move on for further competitions.

hot rod: another name for a drag racing car.

horsepower: a unit of power equal to that produced by one horse and by which engines are rated.

lap: one complete circuit of a racetrack.

logos: an identifying emblem or symbol that provides instant recognition of an object.

NASCAR (National Association for Stock Car Auto Racing): an organization that runs and governs a series of races popular throughout the United States.

Nextel Cup series: a series of races in which the top NASCAR drivers compete.

pit: the area of a racetrack where cars go for tire changes or repairs.

pole position: the place at the front of the starting grid. The car that does best in the preliminary heats gets to start the race in the pole position.

pro-stock: a regular production model of a car that is modified to particpate in races.

resistance: a force that slows progress; the force of the wind pressing against a hard object, such as a car body.

slipstream: the calm area immediately behind a vehicle moving through air or water. Race drivers like to tuck into the slipstream of a leading car to gain speed and use less fuel.

spectators: people watching an event.

starting grid: the place on the racetrack where cars line up to start a race.

streamlined: designed in smooth lines so that wind or water flows easily around the object.

Top Fuel: name given to the fastest type of drag racer.

Index